Do it yourself ANIME.

John Larsen.

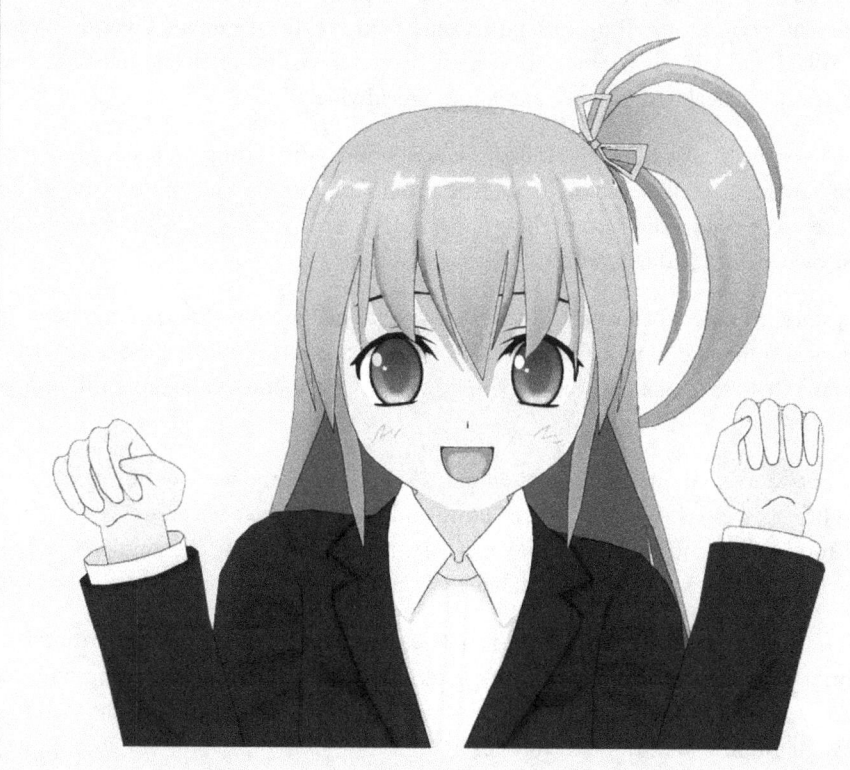

DO IT YOURSELF ANIME.

BY

John Larsen

Welcome to "Do It Yourself Anime"! In this comprehensive guide, we will explore the world of anime from its humble beginnings to the thriving industry it has become today. This book is designed for anyone who wants to learn about anime creation, whether you're an aspiring artist, writer, or just a fan who wants to understand the process better. Throughout the chapters, you'll find helpful tips, step-by-step instructions, and insights into the anime world that will help you develop your skills and bring your own unique anime creations to life.

Anime is a Japanese term that refers to animated works, and it has become a global phenomenon with its distinct art style, storytelling techniques, and memorable characters. Over the years, anime has evolved into various genres and formats, from television series and movies to online streaming platforms, catering to diverse audiences worldwide.

In the first chapter, we'll delve into the foundations of anime, discussing its history and the pioneers who helped shape this exciting medium. From there, we'll move on to essential drawing techniques, character design, and storytelling in anime, giving you the tools you need to start creating your own stories and characters.

We'll also explore the world of manga, the gateway to anime, and how these comic books have inspired countless animated works. Color, backgrounds, and world-building are other critical aspects of anime that we'll tackle, teaching you how to set the mood and breathe life into your creations.

Animation is, of course, an integral part of anime, so we'll cover the basics of bringing your characters to life, as well as the art of voice acting and selecting the perfect voices for your characters. Music and soundtracks also play a crucial role in enhancing the anime experience, and we'll discuss how to choose the right tunes to complement your work.

For those who want to turn their passion into a profession, we'll provide tips on writing the perfect script, navigating the business side of the anime industry, and collaborating with others to build your dream team. Marketing and promoting your anime is another important skill to master, and we'll guide you through the process.

Lastly, we'll look towards the future of anime, exploring new horizons, trends, and opportunities for growth. So, let's embark on this exciting journey together, as you learn how to create your very own anime masterpiece!

Table of Contents

Chapter Titles:

Chapter 1: The Foundations of Anime: A Brief History

Hey there, anime enthusiasts! Welcome to the world of anime, where art meets storytelling in the most delightful way. In this chapter, we'll dive into the foundations of anime, tracing its history from the early days to the global phenomenon it is today. So, buckle up and get ready for a fascinating journey!

A Tale of Beginnings

You might be wondering how it all started. Well, anime's roots can be traced back to the early 20th century in Japan. The first known Japanese animated film, "Katsudō Shashin," was created around 1907 by an unknown artist, and although it only consisted of 50 frames, it was the beginning of something magical.

Fast forward to the 1920s and 1930s, when pioneers like Ōten Shimokawa, Seitarō Kitayama, and Jun'ichi Kōuchi began producing short animated films, many of which were inspired by Western animation, particularly Disney. These works were still relatively simple and lacked the unique features we now associate with anime, but they paved the way for future developments.

Post-War Anime Boom

The Second World War brought about a lot of changes in Japan, including the animation industry. During this time, Japanese artists started creating propaganda films for the government, which led to the growth and development of animation techniques. However, it wasn't until the 1950s and 1960s that the true anime style began to emerge.

Osamu Tezuka, known as the "God of Manga" and the "Walt Disney of Japan," played a critical role in shaping anime as we know it today. His groundbreaking work, "Astro Boy" (known as "Tetsuwan Atomu" in Japan), was the first serialized Japanese TV series that featured distinct characteristics of anime, such as large eyes and exaggerated facial expressions. Tezuka's innovative storytelling and artistic style laid the groundwork for future anime creators.

The 1970s: A Golden Era

The 1970s was a transformative period for anime. Series like "Lupin III" and "Mobile Suit Gundam" not only captured the hearts of Japanese viewers but also started attracting global audiences. These shows introduced complex narratives, well-developed characters, and innovative animation techniques.

During this time, the anime industry also began exploring different genres, such as mecha (giant robots), shōnen (aimed at young boys), and shōjo (aimed at young girls). This diversification helped broaden anime's appeal and led to the creation of several timeless classics.

The 1980s: Home Video Revolution

The 1980s saw the rise of home video, which allowed anime to be distributed on a much larger scale. This led to the production of numerous OVA (Original Video Animation) titles, which were straight-to-video releases. OVAs allowed creators more freedom and often contained more mature content.

Some of the notable OVAs from this period include "Bubblegum Crisis," "Riding Bean," and "Legend of the Galactic Heroes." The 1980s also saw the release of some influential movies, such as Hayao Miyazaki's "My Neighbor Totoro" and Katsuhiro Otomo's "Akira," which pushed the boundaries of animation and storytelling.

The 1990s: The Global Phenomenon

The 1990s were an exciting time for anime, as it started gaining worldwide recognition. Series like "Dragon Ball," "Sailor Moon," and "Neon Genesis Evangelion" became household names and garnered a massive following outside Japan. These shows, along with other popular titles like "Pokémon" and "Cowboy Bebob" introduced anime to a whole new generation of fans.

During this time, the anime industry also experimented with new styles and genres. For instance, "Ghost in the Shell" and "Serial Experiments Lain" explored complex themes, such as the nature of consciousness and the impact of technology on society. Additionally, "Cardcaptor Sakura" and "Revolutionary Girl Utena" broke new ground in the shōjo genre, featuring strong female protagonists and tackling themes like gender identity and self-discovery.

The 2000s: The Digital Age

As we entered the new millennium, the anime industry embraced digital technologies, which brought about a shift in the way animations were produced. The use of digital tools led to higher-quality visuals, more fluid animation, and quicker production times.

The 2000s also saw the rise of online streaming platforms, which made anime more accessible to international audiences. This increased visibility led to a surge in popularity for shows like "Naruto," "Bleach," and "One Piece." These long-running shōnen series had a significant impact on the anime landscape, influencing future creators and captivating fans worldwide.

Moreover, the 2000s gave birth to critically acclaimed anime movies, such as "Spirited Away" by Studio Ghibli and "5 Centimeters Per Second" by Makoto Shinkai. These films further showcased the depth and beauty of anime storytelling, resonating with audiences and earning recognition in international film festivals.

The 2010s: A New Wave of Creativity

The 2010s were marked by a new wave of creativity in the anime industry. This era brought us fresh and innovative titles like "Attack on Titan," "One Punch Man," and "My Hero Academia," which reinvigorated the shōnen genre with their unique twists and memorable characters.

During this time, anime also explored different narrative styles and genres. For instance, "Your Name" by Makoto Shinkai combined romance, drama, and supernatural elements in a visually stunning package, while "Puella Magi Madoka Magica" took the magical girl genre and turned it on its head with a darker, more psychological story.

Furthermore, the 2010s saw the rise of "slice of life" anime, which focused on everyday experiences and relatable situations. Shows like "K-On!" and "March Comes in Like a Lion" captivated audiences with their heartfelt stories and charming characters, proving that anime doesn't always have to be action-packed or fantastical to make an impact.

Present Day and Beyond

Today, anime has become a global phenomenon, enjoyed by millions of fans worldwide. It has grown from its humble beginnings into a diverse and ever-evolving art form, encompassing a wide range of styles, genres, and themes.

With streaming platforms like Crunchyroll and Netflix investing in anime production and distribution, the future looks bright for the industry. As technology continues to advance and the global demand for anime content grows, we can expect to see even more groundbreaking works that challenge conventions and push the boundaries of storytelling and animation.

In conclusion, the foundations of anime have been laid by countless passionate artists and visionaries over the past century. From its early beginnings to its current status as a worldwide sensation, anime has transformed and adapted to the changing times, captivating audiences with its unique blend of art and storytelling. As we look forward to the future, there's no doubt that the world of anime will continue to evolve and inspire generations to come. So, here's to celebrating the rich history of anime and the many amazing adventures yet to unfold!

Chapter 2: Drawing Techniques for Aspiring Anime Artists

Hey there, future anime artists! If you're looking to dive into the world of anime art, you've come to the right place. In this chapter, we'll cover some essential drawing techniques that will help you bring your favorite characters to life on paper. So, grab your sketchbook and let's get started!

Understanding Anime Anatomy

First things first, let's talk about anatomy. While anime characters often have exaggerated features, it's crucial to understand human anatomy to create convincing and visually appealing characters. Here are a few pointers to help you get started:

Study human proportions: A typical adult human figure is around 7-8 head lengths tall, with the legs accounting for roughly half of the total height. Remember that these proportions can vary in anime, but it's essential to maintain a sense of balance and consistency within your style.

Simplify shapes: Break down the human body into simple shapes, like circles for the head and chest and cylinders for the limbs. This will help you grasp the basic structure and make it easier to pose your characters.

Pay attention to joints: Joints, such as the elbows, knees, and wrists, play a critical role in determining how the limbs can bend and move. Make sure to account for these when posing your characters.

Mastering Facial Features

One of the most distinctive aspects of anime art is the characters' facial features. Let's explore how to draw these expressive elements:

Eyes: Anime eyes are often large and expressive, with a variety of shapes and styles. Start by drawing a basic almond shape and then add details like the iris, pupil, and eyelashes. Don't forget the eyebrows, as they can help convey a character's emotions.

Nose: In anime, noses are typically simplified and can range from a single line to a small triangle or wedge shape. Experiment with different styles to find the one that suits your character best.

Mouth: Anime mouths can be as simple as a line or as detailed as you'd like. To convey emotions, pay attention to the shape of the lips and the position of the mouth in relation to the other facial features.

Crafting Unique Hairstyles

Anime hairstyles are often bold and imaginative, with gravity-defying shapes and vibrant colors. Here's how to create captivating hairdos for your characters:

Start with the hairline: Establish the hairline on the forehead, keeping in mind that it can vary depending on the character's age and gender.

Sketch the basic shape: Draw the overall shape of the hairstyle, considering factors like volume, length, and texture. This will serve as a guide for adding details later.

Add strands and details: Once you have the basic shape, begin adding strands of hair and refining the style. Pay attention to how the hair falls and moves to create a sense of flow and realism.

Outfitting Your Characters

Clothing and accessories can help define a character's personality and background. When designing outfits for your characters, consider the following:

Choose a style: Consider the setting and theme of your story when selecting a clothing style. Is it a futuristic sci-fi world or a medieval fantasy realm? Make sure the outfits match the context.

Think about functionality: While it's essential to create visually appealing outfits, don't forget about functionality. Consider how the clothing would affect the character's movement and whether it's practical for their lifestyle or role.

Add accessories: Accessories like weapons, jewelry, or bags can add depth to a character's design and provide visual cues about their background or abilities.

Posing Your Characters

Dynamic poses can make your characters feel more alive and engaging. To create exciting poses, keep these tips in mind:

Use reference images: Don't be afraid to use real-life images or photographs as references for your poses. This can help you understand how the body moves and make your characters feel more believable.

Create a sense of balance: Ensure that your characters have a stable center of gravity to avoid awkward or unnatural poses. Pay attention to how their weight is distributed and how the limbs are positioned.

Add movement and energy: To make your characters feel more dynamic, try incorporating movement and energy into your poses. This can be achieved by using foreshortening, action lines, or even adding motion blur to suggest rapid movement.

Utilizing Shading and Highlights

Adding shading and highlights to your drawings can bring depth and dimension to your characters. Here are a few tips on how to effectively use these techniques:

Determine the light source: Before you start shading, decide on the direction of your light source. This will help you understand where the shadows and highlights should be placed.

Use gradients: When shading, use gradients to create a smooth transition between light and shadow. This can be achieved by gradually varying the pressure of your pencil or using blending tools like smudge sticks or blending stumps.

Add highlights: Highlights are essential for adding a sense of volume to your characters. Use a lighter pencil or an eraser to add highlights on the areas directly facing the light source.

Developing Your Own Style

As you practice and grow as an artist, you'll start to develop your unique style. To help you find your artistic voice, consider these tips:

Study your favorite artists: Look at the works of your favorite anime artists and analyze what you like about their style. Try incorporating some of their techniques into your drawings to see what works for you.

Experiment with different techniques: Don't be afraid to try new things and step out of your comfort zone. This can help you discover techniques and styles that resonate with you.

Keep practicing: Developing your style takes time and patience. Keep drawing and refining your skills, and eventually, your unique artistic voice will emerge.

Utilizing Digital Tools

While traditional drawing tools like pencils and paper are great for learning the basics, many anime artists have transitioned to using digital tools to create their art. Here are some tips for getting started with digital art:

Choose a drawing tablet: If you're serious about digital art, investing in a drawing tablet is essential. There are various options available, ranging from affordable entry-level models to high-end professional devices.

Select a drawing software: There's a wide range of drawing software available, both free and paid. Programs like Clip Studio Paint, Adobe Photoshop, and Paint Tool SAI are popular choices among anime artists. Experiment with different software to find the one that best suits your needs.

Learn digital techniques: Digital art offers unique techniques that you won't find in traditional art, such as layers, filters, and custom brushes. Take the time to learn these tools and techniques to elevate your digital art skills.

In conclusion, learning to draw anime characters is a fun and rewarding journey that requires practice, patience, and persistence. By mastering the basics of anatomy, facial features, hairstyles, clothing, posing, shading, and digital tools, you'll be well on your way to becoming a skilled anime artist. Remember, the key to success is practice and determination, so keep drawing, experimenting, and refining your style. With dedication and passion, you'll undoubtedly see your skills and artistic voice blossom. Happy drawing!

Chapter 3: Character Design: Crafting Memorable Personalities

Hey there, aspiring character designers! In this chapter, we're going to explore the art of creating memorable and engaging anime characters. Designing a character involves more than just drawing cool outfits and hairstyles; it's about developing unique personalities that resonate with audiences. So, grab your sketchbook and let's dive in!

Defining Your Character's Role

Before you start designing your character, it's essential to understand their role within your story. Are they the protagonist, antagonist, or a supporting character? Each role comes with its own set of expectations and conventions, which can help guide your design choices.

Protagonist: The main character of your story, usually someone the audience can relate to or root for. Protagonists often have strong motivations and are faced with challenges they must overcome.

Antagonist: The character that opposes the protagonist and creates conflict within the story. Antagonists can be villains or simply individuals with opposing goals or beliefs.

Supporting Characters: These characters assist or interact with the protagonist and antagonist, adding depth and variety to the story. They can be friends, family, mentors, or even comic relief.

Developing a Backstory

Creating a backstory for your character is crucial, as it helps you understand their motivations, goals, and personality. Consider the following when developing your character's backstory:

Origin: Where does your character come from? How has their upbringing and environment shaped who they are today?

Family and Relationships: Who are your character's family members, and what is their relationship like? How do their relationships with others influence their actions and choices?

Key Experiences: What are the defining moments or experiences in your character's life that have shaped their personality and beliefs?

Crafting a Unique Personality

A memorable character needs a unique and engaging personality. To develop your character's personality, consider the following traits and aspects:

Core Values: What are your character's fundamental beliefs and principles? These values can drive their actions and decisions throughout the story.

Strengths and Weaknesses: What are your character's strengths and weaknesses? Balancing strengths and weaknesses can make your character more relatable and complex.

Hobbies and Interests: What does your character enjoy doing in their spare time? Hobbies and interests can reveal a lot about a character's personality and provide opportunities for character development and storytelling.

Designing the Physical Appearance

Now that you have a solid understanding of your character's backstory and personality, it's time to design their physical appearance. Consider the following factors when creating your character's look:

Age and Body Type: How old is your character, and what body type best suits their personality and role in the story? Remember to keep your character's anatomy consistent and believable, even when exaggerating features for an anime style.

Facial Features: As we discussed in the previous chapter, facial features are a key aspect of anime character design. Experiment with different eye, nose, and mouth shapes to find the perfect combination that reflects your character's personality.

Hairstyle and Color: Choose a hairstyle that complements your character's personality and role in the story. Don't be afraid to experiment with vibrant hair colors and unique styles – this is anime, after all!

Clothing and Accessories: When designing your character's outfit, consider their personality, background, and the story's setting. Think about how their clothing reflects their role in the story and how it might impact their movement and actions.

Using Visual Symbols and Motifs

Incorporating visual symbols and motifs into your character's design can add depth and make them more memorable. Consider the following when adding symbolic elements to your character:

Color Schemes: Colors can convey emotions and personality traits. For example, red might symbolize passion or aggression, while blue can represent calmness or intelligence. Choose a color scheme that reflects your character's personality and role in the story.

Patterns and Details: Adding patterns or details to your character's clothing or accessories can help reinforce their personality or backstory. For instance, a character from a noble background might wear intricate patterns or embroidery, while a warrior might have battle scars or wear armor.

Iconography: Incorporating icons or symbols into your character's design can provide visual cues about their abilities or allegiances. For example, a magical character might have a unique emblem representing their powers, or a character from a specific faction might wear a recognizable insignia.

Creating Emotional Range

A well-rounded character should be able to express a wide range of emotions. To achieve this, practice drawing your character's face with different expressions:

Happiness: Experiment with different types of smiles, from subtle grins to wide, beaming smiles. Pay attention to how the eyes and eyebrows change with the expression.

Sadness: Show your character's sadness through downcast eyes, furrowed brows, or quivering lips. Tears can also be used to convey strong emotions.

Anger: To depict anger, try furrowing the eyebrows, narrowing the eyes, and clenching the jaw. You can also experiment with more exaggerated expressions, like bulging veins or gritted teeth.

Surprise or Fear: Widen the eyes and raise the eyebrows to show surprise or fear. The mouth can be open, gasping, or screaming, depending on the intensity of the emotion.

Consistency in Design

When designing a cast of characters, it's essential to maintain consistency in style and proportions. This helps create a unified look for your story and makes it easier for the audience to identify and connect with your characters. To ensure consistency:

Use a reference sheet: Create a reference sheet for each character that includes their front, side, and back views, as well as close-ups of their face and any important details or accessories. This will help you maintain consistency when drawing your characters from different angles or in various scenes.

Stick to your style: Whether you're going for a realistic or more stylized approach, make sure to apply the same artistic style to all of your characters. This creates visual harmony and helps establish a recognizable look for your story.

Check proportions: Ensure that your characters' proportions remain consistent across different poses and scenes. Use guidelines or a grid to help maintain proper proportions and alignment.

Testing Your Character Design

Once you've designed your character, it's crucial to test their design in various contexts to ensure they work well within your story. Consider the following:

Dynamic Poses: Draw your character in a variety of poses to see how their design holds up in different situations. This can help you identify any issues with clothing, accessories, or anatomy that might need adjustments.

Interactions: Sketch your character interacting with other characters or objects from your story. This can help you gauge how well their design works within the context of your story and whether any changes need to be made.

Storyboarding: Create rough storyboards or comic panels featuring your character to see how their design translates to a narrative format. This can help you spot any inconsistencies or issues with their design that might not be apparent in standalone illustrations.

In conclusion, crafting memorable and engaging anime characters involves developing a strong backstory, unique personality, and visually appealing design. By considering your character's role, backstory, personality, physical appearance, emotional range, and consistency, you can create characters that resonate with audiences and bring your story to life. Remember, practice makes perfect, so keep refining your character designs and exploring new ideas to develop your unique artistic voice. With dedication and passion, you'll be able to create unforgettable characters that captivate your audience and enrich your storytelling.

Evolving Your Characters

As your story progresses, it's natural for your characters to grow and evolve. This growth can be reflected in both their personalities and their physical appearances. To effectively showcase your characters' development, consider the following:

Updating Outfits: Changing a character's outfit can be a visual cue of their growth or progression in the story. This can include upgrading their armor, adopting a new style, or even simply changing their wardrobe to reflect their evolving tastes and interests.

Physical Changes: Sometimes, a character's development can be shown through physical changes, such as scars, tattoos, or changes in hairstyle. These changes can serve as reminders of their experiences and personal growth throughout the story.

Emotional Growth: As your characters face challenges and learn from their experiences, their personalities and emotional range may also evolve. Be sure to incorporate these changes into your character design and expressions, showcasing their newfound wisdom, confidence, or vulnerability.

Creating Diverse and Inclusive Characters

In today's globalized world, it's essential to create diverse and inclusive characters that represent a wide range of cultures, backgrounds, and experiences. This not only makes your story more engaging and relatable but also helps promote understanding and empathy among your audience. Here are some tips for creating diverse and inclusive characters:

Research: If you're designing a character from a culture or background that you're not familiar with, do thorough research to ensure authenticity and avoid perpetuating stereotypes. Consult reputable sources, and if possible, consult people from the culture you're representing.

Avoid Stereotypes: Be mindful of stereotypes and clichés when creating characters from diverse backgrounds. Aim to create complex and nuanced characters that challenge conventional representations and break away from harmful stereotypes.

Representation Matters: Ensure that your cast of characters represents a diverse range of backgrounds, abilities, and experiences. This can help create a richer and more engaging story, as well as encourage empathy and understanding among your audience.

In summary, designing memorable and engaging anime characters is a rewarding and creative process that requires a deep understanding of the characters' roles, backstories, personalities, and physical appearances. By focusing on emotional range, consistency, character growth, and diversity, you'll be able to create captivating characters that bring your story to life. Remember to practice, experiment, and stay true to your artistic vision as you continue to refine your skills and develop your unique style. Happy character designing!

Chapter 4: Storytelling in Anime: Building Compelling Narratives

Hey there, aspiring anime creators! Welcome to Chapter 4, where we'll be talking about the heart of any great anime: storytelling. A compelling narrative can make or break your anime, so let's dive into the nitty-gritty of building a story that'll have your audience hooked!

Start with a strong concept

First up, you need a killer concept that'll form the backbone of your story. This can be anything from an epic adventure to a heartwarming slice-of-life tale. Think about what interests you and what kind of stories you enjoy watching. Keep in mind that your concept should be unique and engaging to stand out in the world of anime.

Develop memorable characters

Characters are the lifeblood of your story, so make sure they're well-rounded and relatable. Start by creating a diverse cast with different backgrounds, personalities, and motivations. Flesh out their histories, their quirks, and how they interact with one another. Don't be afraid to give your characters flaws; it makes them more human and adds depth to your story.

Craft an engaging plot

With your concept and characters in place, it's time to create a plot that keeps viewers on the edge of their seats. Break your story down into three acts: the beginning, middle, and end. The beginning should introduce your characters and set up the main conflict. In the middle, the characters should face challenges and develop as they try to resolve the conflict. The end should bring everything to a satisfying conclusion, with the characters having grown and changed through their experiences.

Keep the pacing in check

Pacing is crucial in maintaining your audience's interest. Too slow, and they'll get bored; too fast, and they'll struggle to keep up. Strike a balance by varying the tempo of your story. Mix intense action scenes with quieter moments of character development. This creates a natural rhythm that keeps viewers engaged and eager to see what happens next.

Embrace themes and symbolism

Great storytelling often goes beyond surface-level plotlines, touching on deeper themes and symbolism that resonate with viewers. Think about the underlying message you want to convey and how to weave it throughout your story. This can be done through visual motifs, dialogue, character development, or even the plot itself. Adding layers of meaning to your anime will make it more thought-provoking and memorable.

Create a unique setting

A captivating setting can immerse viewers in your story and make it feel more alive. Whether it's a futuristic city or a magical fantasy realm, take the time to build a detailed and visually stunning world. Consider the culture, history, and geography of your setting, and how they impact the story and characters. The more immersive your world, the more invested your audience will be in your story.

Use effective storytelling techniques

Anime offers a unique medium for visual storytelling. Leverage the power of animation to convey emotions, establish atmosphere, and depict action. Experiment with different camera angles, lighting, and color schemes to create a unique visual style that complements your story. Additionally, consider using techniques like flashbacks, foreshadowing, and symbolism to add depth and intrigue to your narrative.

Make your dialogue count

Dialogue is a vital tool for character development and story progression. Keep your conversations natural and engaging, avoiding long-winded monologues or stilted exchanges. Each line should have a purpose, whether it's revealing information, developing relationships, or showing a character's personality. Remember to balance dialogue with visual storytelling, using both in tandem to create a rich, immersive experience.

Take inspiration from different sources

While it's essential to develop your own unique voice, there's nothing wrong

----

Chapter 5: The World of Manga - A Gateway to Anime

Hey there, fellow anime enthusiasts! Welcome to Chapter 5, where we'll explore the fascinating world of manga and how it serves as a gateway to anime. Manga, the Japanese art of comics and graphic novels, has a long and rich history that's deeply intertwined with anime. So let's dive right in and see how this captivating medium can inspire and enhance your anime journey!

Understanding the roots of manga

To fully appreciate manga's impact on anime, it's essential to know its roots. Manga has been around since the late 19th century, but it really took off after World War II, thanks to artists like Osamu Tezuka, known as the "godfather of manga." Tezuka's groundbreaking work, Astro Boy, was later adapted into one of the earliest successful anime series. Since then, countless manga titles have been transformed into hit anime, creating a vibrant feedback loop between the two mediums.

Manga genres and demographics

Manga caters to a wide range of tastes, with genres and subgenres spanning everything from action-packed shonen and magical girl tales to introspective seinen and heartwarming josei stories. This diverse array of storytelling styles offers a wealth of inspiration for anime creators, allowing you to explore new ideas and themes that might be less prevalent in existing anime.

Adapting manga to anime

Many successful anime series are based on manga, and adapting a manga story to the screen can be a fantastic way to bring your vision to life. When adapting a manga, consider the pacing, visual style, and character development, making sure they translate effectively to the animated medium. It's essential to strike a balance between staying faithful to the source material and making necessary changes to create a compelling anime adaptation.

How manga can improve your visual storytelling

Manga is a visual storytelling medium that relies on a combination of static images and text to convey its narrative. Studying manga can teach you valuable lessons in visual storytelling, such as how to compose dynamic panels, use visual cues to convey emotion, and establish a consistent art style. These skills can prove invaluable when it comes to creating visually stunning and engaging anime.

Manga as a storyboard

Manga can serve as an excellent starting point for developing your anime storyboard. By studying the panel layouts, camera angles, and visual storytelling techniques used in manga, you can learn how to create impactful and well-paced storyboards that translate seamlessly to the screen.

Exploring manga's unique visual language

Manga has its own visual language, using symbols and visual cues to express emotions, thoughts, and actions. For example, "speed lines" are used to convey motion, while "chibi" characters represent a lighthearted or comedic moment. Incorporating these manga-inspired visual elements into your anime can add a unique flair and help convey your story's tone and mood.

Creating original manga as a stepping stone to anime

If you're an aspiring anime creator who's also skilled at drawing, consider creating an original manga as a stepping stone to anime. By developing your story and characters through manga, you can establish a fanbase, gather feedback, and refine your ideas before embarking on the more complex and time-consuming process of creating an anime.

Collaborating with manga artists

Collaborating with manga artists can be a fantastic way to bring your anime vision to life. A skilled manga artist can help you develop your story, create visually striking character designs and backgrounds, and assist with storyboarding. This partnership can result in a cohesive and visually stunning anime that truly captures the essence of your story.

The importance of respecting the source material

When adapting a manga into an anime, it's crucial to respect the source material and stay true to its spirit. This means maintaining the essence of the characters, story, and visual style, while also making necessary adaptations for the animated medium. Fans of the original manga will appreciate your dedication to the source material, and newcomers will benefit from a well-crafted adaptation that captures the heart of the story.

Learning from successful manga-to-anime adaptations

There are numerous examples of successful manga-to-anime adaptations that you can learn from. Series like Naruto, One Piece, Attack on Titan, and My Hero Academia have managed to captivate audiences through their faithful adaptations, compelling storytelling, and striking visuals. Analyze these adaptations to gain insight into what works and what doesn't when translating a manga to the screen. This will help you avoid common pitfalls and create a winning adaptation of your own.

Embracing the creative freedom of anime

While it's essential to respect the source material, don't forget that anime offers unique creative opportunities that can enhance the story. With animation, you can depict action scenes more dynamically, explore unique color palettes and lighting techniques, and add an extra layer of depth with voice acting and music. Use the animated medium to its fullest potential to create a memorable and immersive experience for your viewers.

The power of manga as a marketing tool

Manga can also serve as a powerful marketing tool for your anime. By creating a manga adaptation of your anime, or vice versa, you can expand your audience and generate buzz for your project. A popular manga series can draw attention to your anime and help it gain traction, while an anime adaptation of a manga can bring in new fans who might not have otherwise discovered the original source material.

Staying inspired by reading and watching

To stay inspired and informed about the world of manga and anime, make a habit of regularly reading manga and watching anime. This will expose you to a wide variety of storytelling styles, visual techniques, and genres, helping you hone your skills as a creator. You'll also stay up-to-date with the latest trends and innovations in the industry, giving you a competitive edge in the ever-evolving world of anime and manga.

Connecting with the manga and anime community

Finally, don't forget the importance of connecting with fellow fans and creators in the manga and anime community. Attend conventions, join online forums, and participate in social media discussions to network with like-minded individuals, share your work, and gather valuable feedback. Engaging with the community can lead to valuable collaborations, friendships, and a deeper understanding of the art forms you love.

In conclusion, the world of manga serves as a vital gateway to anime, offering a wealth of inspiration, storytelling techniques, and visual language unique to the medium. By understanding the roots of manga, studying successful adaptations, and embracing the creative opportunities offered by both manga and anime, you'll be well-equipped to create captivating stories that resonate with audiences and leave a lasting impact.

So there you have it! A deep dive into the world of manga and its connection to anime. Now, armed with this knowledge, you're ready to take your anime creation journey to the next level. Happy creating!

Chapter 6: The Power of Color: Setting the Mood and Tone

Hey there, creative folks! Welcome to Chapter 6, where we'll explore the power of color in anime and how it can be used to set the mood and tone of your story. The right color palette can evoke emotions, enhance atmosphere, and breathe life into your characters and settings. So, let's dive in and learn how to harness the power of color to create a visually stunning and emotionally impactful anime!

Understanding color theory

Before you start splashing colors all over your anime, it's essential to understand the basics of color theory. Color theory is the study of how colors interact, complement, and contrast with one another. Familiarize yourself with the color wheel, primary, secondary, and tertiary colors, as well as concepts like hue, saturation, and value. A solid grasp of color theory will help you create harmonious and visually appealing color schemes for your anime.

Choosing a color palette

Once you have a handle on color theory, it's time to choose a color palette for your anime. This palette should reflect the mood and tone of your story, as well as the personalities of your characters and the environments they inhabit. Consider using a limited color palette to create a cohesive and distinctive look for your anime. Experiment with different combinations of colors until you find the perfect balance that captures the essence of your story.

Setting the mood with color

Color has a powerful impact on our emotions, and as an anime creator, you can use this to your advantage. By carefully selecting your colors, you can evoke specific feelings and create a particular atmosphere. For example, warm colors like red, orange, and yellow can evoke feelings of excitement, passion, and energy, while cool colors like blue, green, and purple can convey calmness, serenity, and mystery. Consider the emotional response you want to elicit from your audience, and choose your colors accordingly.

Using color to define characters

Colors can also be used to enhance your characters' personalities and make them more visually distinctive. Assigning each character a specific color or color scheme can help them stand out and be easily recognizable. Additionally, the colors you choose can convey information about a character's personality, alignment, or emotional state. For example, a hero might be associated with bright, bold colors, while a villain could be linked to darker, more muted tones.

Creating atmosphere through color

Color plays a crucial role in establishing the atmosphere of your anime. By using specific color palettes, you can create a sense of time, place, and mood. For example, a scene set at night might use deep blues and purples to create a sense of darkness and mystery, while a sunny day scene could be filled with bright, vibrant colors that evoke warmth and happiness. Be mindful of the atmosphere you want to create and use color to enhance that feeling.

Color grading and post-processing

Color grading is the process of adjusting the colors and tones of your finished animation to achieve a specific look or mood. This can involve changing the brightness, contrast, and saturation, as well as adding filters or color overlays. Color grading can make a significant difference in the final appearance of your anime, so don't overlook its importance. Experiment with different color grading techniques in post-processing to find the perfect look for your project.

Using color symbolism

Color symbolism is the practice of using colors to represent specific ideas, emotions, or themes. In anime, color symbolism can be used to convey deeper meanings or add layers of complexity to your story. For example, red might symbolize passion or danger, while green could represent growth or renewal. Be aware of the cultural context of the colors you choose, as color symbolism can vary between different cultures and regions. By incorporating color symbolism into your anime, you can add depth and intrigue to your storytelling.

Color and visual storytelling

Colors can be used to enhance visual storytelling by guiding the viewer's attention and emphasizing important elements within a scene. For instance, a bright color amidst a more muted background can draw attention to a specific character or object. Similarly, using contrasting colors can emphasize the difference between characters, factions, or environments. Experiment with color placement to strengthen your visual storytelling and ensure your audience focuses on the key elements of your story.

Color consistency

Maintaining color consistency throughout your anime is essential for creating a cohesive visual experience. This means using the same color palette and style across different scenes, characters, and environments. Consistency helps establish a recognizable visual identity for your anime and makes it more memorable for your audience. Of course, you can still use variations in color to highlight specific moments or convey changes in mood, but make sure these changes are deliberate and support your overall narrative.

Studying color in existing anime

To gain a better understanding of how color is used in anime, study existing works that have made effective use of color. Analyze how these anime use color palettes to create mood, convey character personalities, and enhance visual storytelling. Take note of the techniques employed and consider how you can apply these lessons to your own project. Some excellent examples of anime with exceptional use of color include Studio Ghibli films, Your Name, and Demon Slayer.

Collaboration with your team

Creating a visually stunning and emotionally impactful anime is a collaborative effort. Work closely with your animation team, including character designers, background artists, and colorists, to ensure that your vision for the color palette is executed consistently and effectively. Share your ideas, listen to their input, and be open to experimentation. A strong collaborative environment will result in a final product that truly shines.

Continuously learning and evolving

As with any creative skill, mastering the use of color in anime requires continuous learning and practice. Keep exploring new ideas, techniques, and color palettes to expand your repertoire and improve your skills. Stay informed about the latest trends and innovations in the world of color and animation, and be open to adapting your style as you grow as a creator.

In conclusion, the power of color in setting the mood and tone of your anime cannot be overstated. By understanding color theory, choosing the right color palette, and employing techniques like color symbolism and visual storytelling, you can create an anime that captivates your audience and leaves a lasting impression. So go forth, experiment with color, and watch your anime come to life in a vibrant, emotional, and visually stunning way!

Chapter 7: Backgrounds and World-Building: Breathing Life into Your Anime

Hey there, anime enthusiasts! Welcome to Chapter 7, where we'll delve into the art of backgrounds and world-building in anime. A well-developed world and detailed backgrounds can make your anime feel alive, immersive, and truly unforgettable. So, let's jump in and learn how to create captivating environments that will transport your audience to the heart of your anime universe!

The importance of backgrounds

Backgrounds are an essential aspect of anime that should never be overlooked. They provide the setting for your story, create a sense of depth and scale, and help establish the atmosphere and mood of each scene. By investing time and effort into crafting detailed and engaging backgrounds, you can make your anime feel more immersive and visually appealing.

The basics of world-building

World-building is the process of creating a unique and believable setting for your anime. This involves defining the physical geography, history, culture, and society of your world, as well as the rules that govern it. Start by brainstorming ideas for your world and sketching out rough maps and concept art. As you develop your world, consider how these various elements will impact your story and characters.

Integrating story and world-building

A successful anime seamlessly integrates its story and world-building, with each element informing and enhancing the other. Consider how the history, culture, and society of your world shape your characters and their motivations. Likewise, think about how your characters interact with and are influenced by their environment. By weaving your story and world-building together, you can create a richer, more engaging narrative.

Balancing detail and simplicity

When creating backgrounds and building your world, it's crucial to strike a balance between detail and simplicity. While intricate backgrounds can add depth and visual interest to your anime, they can also become overwhelming or distracting if not executed properly. Keep in mind that your characters and story should always take center stage. Use detail strategically to draw attention to important elements and create a sense of atmosphere without detracting from the main action.

Developing a visual style for your backgrounds

Your backgrounds should have a consistent visual style that complements the overall aesthetic of your anime. Experiment with different techniques, such as hand-painted backgrounds, digital art, or a combination of both, to find the style that best suits your project. Look to existing anime for inspiration, and don't be afraid to develop your own unique approach.

Establishing a sense of scale and depth

One of the most important aspects of background art in anime is creating a sense of scale and depth. This can be achieved through the use of perspective, layering, and atmospheric effects like haze or color grading. Study the principles of perspective and practice drawing scenes with varying levels of depth to hone your skills in this area. Additionally, consider how your characters interact with their environment to further enhance the sense of scale and depth in your scenes.

Creating immersive environments

To create truly immersive environments, pay attention to the small details that bring a setting to life. This might include natural elements like plants, animals, and weather, as well as man-made features like architecture, signage, and vehicles. By incorporating these details into your backgrounds, you can create a world that feels lived-in and authentic.

Utilizing lighting and color

Lighting and color are essential tools for setting the mood and atmosphere of a scene. Use warm, soft lighting to create a sense of comfort and intimacy, or harsh, contrasting shadows to evoke tension and unease. Likewise, experiment with color to convey different emotions and time periods. By mastering the use of lighting and color in your backgrounds, you can guide your audience's emotional response and enhance the overall impact of your anime.

Incorporating movement and dynamism

Adding movement and dynamism to your backgrounds can make your anime feel more lively and engaging. This can be achieved through the use of parallax scrolling, where different layers of the background move at different speeds to create a sense of depth and motion. You can also incorporate elements like flowing water, rustling leaves, or billowing smoke to add life to your scenes. Remember, though, not to go overboard with movement, as it can become distracting if not used judiciously.

Adapting real-world locations and architecture

Drawing inspiration from real-world locations and architecture can add a layer of authenticity and believability to your anime backgrounds. Study photographs, travel to different locations, or take inspiration from existing architectural styles to create unique and visually interesting settings for your story. Be mindful of cultural context and ensure that your adaptations are respectful and well-researched.

Creating a sense of progression and change

As your story unfolds, it's important to show progression and change in your backgrounds to reflect the passage of time and the development of your characters. This can be achieved by subtly altering the appearance of your settings, such as showing a town gradually being rebuilt after a disaster or the seasons changing throughout your story. By visually representing these changes, you can create a more immersive and dynamic narrative.

Consistency in your world-building

Maintaining consistency in your world-building is crucial for creating a believable and immersive setting. Establish rules and guidelines for your world, and ensure that your backgrounds and environments adhere to these principles. Inconsistencies in your world-building can break the suspension of disbelief and undermine the overall impact of your anime.

Collaboration with your team

Creating detailed and engaging backgrounds is a collaborative effort that involves working closely with your animation team, including background artists, layout artists, and colorists. Communicate your vision clearly and be open to input and suggestions from your team members. By fostering a collaborative environment, you can ensure that your backgrounds are executed effectively and contribute to the overall success of your anime.

Continually learning and improving

As with any creative skill, mastering the art of backgrounds and world-building requires ongoing learning and practice. Study the work of other animators and artists, attend workshops and classes, and seek feedback from your peers to continually refine your skills and develop your unique style. Stay informed about the latest trends and innovations in the world of animation, and be open to adapting your approach as you grow as a creator.

In conclusion, backgrounds and world-building are vital components of successful anime, providing a rich and immersive setting for your characters and story. By understanding the importance of these elements and developing your skills in creating detailed, visually engaging environments, you can breathe life into your anime and transport your audience to a captivating world. So, grab your sketchbook or digital tablet, and start creating the universe your characters call home!

Chapter 8: Animation Basics: Bringing Your Characters to Life

Hey there, future animators! In this chapter, we're diving into the exciting world of animation, where you'll learn how to bring your characters to life and make them move in a way that's both believable and captivating. Animation is a crucial element of any anime, so let's get started with the basics and help you become an animation pro!

Understanding the principles of animation

To create smooth and engaging animation, it's essential to understand the 12 principles of animation, which were developed by Disney animators Frank Thomas and Ollie Johnston. These principles are the foundation of successful animation and will help you create lifelike and appealing character movement. The 12 principles are:

a. Squash and stretch

b. Anticipation

c. Staging

d. Straight ahead action and pose to pose

e. Follow through and overlapping action

f. Slow in and slow out

g. Arcs

h. Secondary action

i. Timing

j. Exaggeration

k. Solid drawing

l. Appeal

Study each principle in-depth and practice applying them to your animations to develop a strong understanding of how they contribute to the overall quality of your work.

Creating keyframes and in-betweens

Keyframes are the main poses or positions of your character that define their movement within a scene. In-betweens are the frames that fill in the gaps between keyframes, creating smooth and fluid movement. Start by drawing your keyframes, then add in-betweens to complete the animation. Remember to apply the principles of animation to your keyframes and in-betweens to ensure your character's movements are believable and engaging.

Working with timing and spacing

Timing refers to the number of frames it takes for an action to occur, while spacing is the distance between the positions of a character in consecutive frames. Both timing and spacing are crucial for creating the illusion of movement and should be carefully considered when planning your animation. Adjust the timing and spacing of your frames to convey different emotions, speeds, and types of movement. For example, a character moving quickly would have fewer frames and larger spacing, while a slow movement would have more frames and smaller spacing.

Emphasizing poses and expressions

Strong poses and expressions can help convey your character's emotions, intentions, and personality. Spend time perfecting your character's key poses and expressions, ensuring they are clear, impactful, and consistent with their personality. By creating expressive and dynamic poses, you can make your animation more engaging and emotionally resonant.

Animating walk cycles and other common actions

Walk cycles and other common actions, such as running, jumping, and sitting, are essential skills for any animator. Practice animating these actions using reference material, such as videos or live models, to develop a strong understanding of how the human body moves in different situations. Once you've mastered these basic actions, experiment with adding personality and style to make them unique to your character.

Creating smooth transitions

Smooth transitions between different actions and poses are vital for maintaining the flow and believability of your animation. Pay close attention to how your character moves from one pose to another and ensure that the transitions are fluid and natural. Use the principles of animation, such as anticipation and follow-through, to help create seamless transitions and maintain the overall quality of your work.

Experimenting with different animation techniques

There are various animation techniques to explore, including hand-drawn animation, digital 2D animation, and 3D animation. Experiment with different techniques and tools to find the style that best suits your project and personal preferences. Each technique has its unique strengths and challenges, so be prepared to invest time and effort into learning and mastering the one that resonates with you the most.

Collaborating with your animation team

Creating an anime is often a collaborative effort, involving a team of animators, artists, and other creative professionals. Learn to work effectively with your team, communicating your ideas clearly and being open to feedback and suggestions. By fostering a positive and cooperative working environment, you'll ensure that your project runs smoothly and your animation is of the highest quality.

Studying the work of other animators

One of the best ways to learn and improve as an animator is to study the work of others. Watch a variety of anime and pay close attention to the animation techniques and styles employed by different artists. Analyze their work and try to identify the principles of animation in action. By learning from the successes and mistakes of others, you can refine your own skills and develop your unique style.

Practice, practice, practice!

As with any creative skill, becoming a proficient animator takes time, dedication, and practice. Set aside regular time to work on your animation skills, experimenting with different techniques, tools, and styles. Seek feedback from your peers and mentors, and be open to criticism and suggestions for improvement. By continually learning and growing as an animator, you'll be well on your way to creating captivating and dynamic anime.

The importance of sound and music

Don't forget that sound and music play a crucial role in bringing your animations to life. Work closely with sound designers and composers to create a soundtrack that enhances your character's movements and emotions. Consider the timing of sound effects and music, ensuring that they sync up with your animation and help to create a cohesive and immersive experience for your audience.

Overcoming challenges and setbacks

Throughout your animation journey, you'll undoubtedly encounter challenges and setbacks. It's essential to maintain a positive mindset and view these obstacles as opportunities for growth and learning. Stay persistent, practice regularly, and continue to develop your skills, and you'll soon see improvement in your work and overcome any hurdles you may face.

In conclusion, mastering the art of animation is a rewarding and essential skill for any aspiring anime creator. By understanding the principles of animation, practicing key techniques, and continually learning from your experiences and the work of others, you'll be well on your way to bringing your characters to life and creating unforgettable, engaging anime. So, grab your drawing tools or fire up your favorite animation software, and start animating your way to success!

Chapter 9: The Art of Voice Acting: Choosing the Perfect Voice for Your Characters

Hey there, anime enthusiasts! In this chapter, we'll be exploring the world of voice acting and how it can make or break your anime. Choosing the perfect voice for your characters is an essential part of the production process, as it helps bring your story to life and creates a connection between your audience and the characters on screen. So, let's dive into the art of voice acting and learn how to select the ideal voices for your characters!

Understanding the importance of voice acting

Voice acting plays a crucial role in the success of any anime, as it helps convey the emotions, personality, and intentions of your characters. A skilled voice actor can breathe life into your characters, making them feel authentic and relatable. Moreover, the right voice can enhance the overall atmosphere and emotional impact of your anime, so it's essential to choose your voice actors wisely.

Defining your characters' vocal qualities

Before you start auditioning voice actors, it's essential to have a clear understanding of your characters' vocal qualities. Consider factors such as their age, gender, personality, and role in the story, as these will influence the type of voice you're looking for. Create a detailed character profile for each role, including vocal characteristics and any specific accents or speech patterns that may be required.

Holding auditions and casting calls

Once you have a clear idea of the vocal qualities you're looking for, it's time to hold auditions and casting calls. Advertise your casting call through social media, online forums, and local acting communities, clearly outlining the roles you're casting and any specific requirements. Be prepared to review many auditions, as finding the perfect voice for your characters can be a time-consuming process.

Preparing audition scripts and materials

To ensure a successful audition process, provide your prospective voice actors with audition scripts and materials that accurately represent your characters and the tone of your anime. This could include a brief character description, a selection of key lines, and some guidance on the emotional context of the scene. Encourage your voice actors to experiment with different approaches and emphasize that you're open to creative interpretations.

Evaluating auditions

When reviewing auditions, pay close attention to the actor's ability to convey the emotions, personality, and nuances of your character. Consider factors such as vocal range, tone, and clarity, as well as their ability to deliver lines with the appropriate pacing and emphasis. Keep an open mind and be prepared to revise your initial vocal expectations if you find a voice actor that brings something unique and engaging to the role.

Communication and direction

Once you've selected your voice actors, it's essential to establish clear communication and provide direction to ensure their performances align with your vision. Share your character profiles and any relevant background information, and discuss your expectations and goals for their performance. Be open to collaboration and encourage your voice actors to contribute their ideas and insights, as this can lead to a more nuanced and authentic performance.

Recording sessions and retakes

During recording sessions, provide your voice actors with guidance and feedback, ensuring their performances are consistent with the tone and style of your anime. Be prepared to request multiple takes and retakes, as even the most experienced voice actors may require several attempts to capture the perfect delivery. Remember to be patient and supportive, as a positive and collaborative working environment will yield the best results.

Syncing voice to animation

Once you have your voice recordings, it's time to sync them with your animation. This can be a challenging process, as it requires precise timing and attention to detail. Work closely with your animation team to ensure the voice and visuals are seamlessly integrated, adjusting the timing and pacing of your animation if necessary to accommodate the voice acting. Keep in mind that sometimes, it may be necessary to request additional recording sessions to fine-tune the synchronization.

Choosing voice actors for multiple languages

If you plan to release your anime in multiple languages, you'll need to cast voice actors for each language version. When selecting voice actors for different languages, strive to maintain consistency in the vocal qualities and characteristics of your characters. This will ensure that your characters remain relatable and authentic, regardless of the language they're speaking.

Working with voice acting agencies

Collaborating with voice acting agencies can be an efficient way to find talented voice actors for your project. Agencies typically have a roster of experienced actors and can help you find the perfect match for your characters. When working with an agency, provide them with detailed character profiles and audition materials to ensure they can recommend suitable candidates for your roles.

Understanding the legal aspects

When hiring voice actors, it's important to be aware of the legal aspects, such as contracts, royalties, and usage rights. Work with a legal advisor to draft contracts that clearly outline the terms of the agreement, including payment, deadlines, and any potential royalties. Ensuring that all parties understand their rights and responsibilities will help prevent any disputes or misunderstandings down the line.

Celebrating your voice actors

Your voice actors play a vital role in bringing your anime to life, so don't forget to acknowledge and celebrate their contributions. Include them in promotional materials, interviews, and events, and give them credit in the end titles of your anime. By showing appreciation for their hard work and talent, you'll foster a positive working relationship and encourage them to continue delivering outstanding performances.

In conclusion, choosing the perfect voice for your characters is a crucial element of creating a successful anime. By carefully considering the vocal qualities of your characters, holding auditions, and providing clear direction and feedback, you can bring your story to life with engaging and authentic voice acting. Remember, the right voice can make all the difference, so take your time and select your voice actors wisely. Happy casting!

Chapter 10: Soundtracks and Music: Complementing Your Anime's Aesthetic

Hey there, fellow anime creators! In this chapter, we'll be exploring the essential role of soundtracks and music in your anime. A well-crafted soundtrack can elevate your story, set the mood, and create memorable moments that will stick with your audience long after the credits roll. So, let's dive into the world of music and learn how to create a soundtrack that perfectly complements your anime's aesthetic!

Understanding the role of music in anime

Music plays a pivotal role in any anime, as it helps to establish the atmosphere, tone, and emotional context of each scene. A skillfully composed soundtrack can enhance the impact of your story, heighten tension, and evoke powerful emotions in your audience. Additionally, memorable opening and closing theme songs can become iconic elements of your anime, contributing to its overall appeal and popularity.

Defining your anime's musical style

To create a cohesive and engaging soundtrack, it's crucial to define the musical style that best suits your anime's aesthetic. Consider the genre, setting, and overall tone of your story, and explore different musical styles and genres that could effectively convey the desired atmosphere.

This could range from orchestral scores for epic fantasy anime to electronic music for futuristic sci-fi settings.

Collaborating with composers and musicians

Creating a captivating soundtrack requires collaboration with talented composers and musicians. Seek out professionals whose work aligns with your anime's musical style and share your vision and goals for the soundtrack. Establish open communication and provide guidance on the emotional context of each scene, ensuring that the music effectively complements your story.

Creating memorable opening and closing themes

The opening and closing themes of your anime are crucial elements that set the stage for your story and leave a lasting impression on your audience. When creating these themes, focus on crafting catchy melodies and meaningful lyrics that encapsulate the essence of your anime. Collaborate with skilled composers, lyricists, and vocalists to bring your themes to life, ensuring that they are both memorable and engaging.

Timing and pacing

When integrating music into your anime, pay close attention to the timing and pacing of each scene. The music should seamlessly flow with the visuals, enhancing the emotional impact without overpowering the dialogue or sound effects. Work closely with your composer and sound designer to ensure that the music is appropriately timed and paced, creating a harmonious balance between the various audio elements.

Using leitmotifs and recurring themes

Leitmotifs and recurring musical themes can be powerful storytelling tools that help to create a sense of continuity and emotional resonance throughout your anime. Consider using recurring motifs to represent specific characters, locations, or emotional states, subtly weaving them into your soundtrack to enhance your story's narrative structure and emotional impact.

Balancing music with sound effects and dialogue

A successful anime soundtrack strikes a careful balance between music, sound effects, and dialogue. Ensure that the music doesn't drown out important dialogue or sound effects, and adjust the volume levels as needed to maintain clarity and audibility. Collaborate with your sound designer to create a cohesive and immersive soundscape that effectively supports your story.

Licensing and legal considerations

When using music in your anime, it's essential to be aware of licensing and legal considerations. If you're working with a composer, ensure that you have a clear agreement outlining the terms of usage and any potential royalties. Additionally, if you plan to use existing music, ensure that you obtain the necessary licenses and permissions to avoid copyright infringement.

The power of silence

While music is an important aspect of your anime's soundscape, don't underestimate the power of silence. Strategic use of silence can create tension, emphasize dramatic moments, and provide contrast to the music and sound effects. By incorporating moments of silence into your soundtrack, you can heighten the emotional impact and create a more dynamic and engaging audio experience for your audience.

Experimenting with unconventional musical elements

Don't be afraid to think outside the box and experiment with unconventional musical elements in your anime's soundtrack. Unique and unexpected musical choices can help to set your anime apart and create a distinct atmosphere that resonates with your audience. Consider incorporating non-traditional instruments, soundscapes, or even silence to create a truly unique and captivating soundtrack.

Building an emotional connection through music

Music has the power to evoke strong emotions and create lasting connections with your audience. Use your soundtrack to reinforce the emotional arcs of your characters and story, ensuring that the music aligns with the mood and tone of each scene. By skillfully weaving music into the fabric of your anime, you can create a deeply immersive and emotionally resonant experience for your viewers.

Curating and releasing your soundtrack

Once you have completed your soundtrack, consider curating and releasing it as a standalone product. This can help to build interest and anticipation for your anime, as well as provide an additional revenue stream. Collaborate with your composer and musicians to create a polished and cohesive album, and promote it through social media, online platforms, and other marketing channels.

In conclusion, a carefully crafted soundtrack can significantly enhance your anime's aesthetic and create a lasting impression on your audience. By defining your anime's musical style, collaborating with talented composers and musicians, and skillfully integrating music into your story, you can create a captivating and emotionally resonant experience that will keep your viewers coming back for more. So, get those creative juices flowing and start composing the perfect soundtrack for your anime masterpiece!

Chapter 11: Tips for Aspiring Anime Writers: Crafting the Perfect Script

Hey there, future anime writers! In this chapter, we'll be diving into the fascinating world of scriptwriting and exploring the essential skills and techniques you'll need to create a captivating anime script. Writing an engaging script is the foundation of any successful anime, so let's get started on your journey to becoming an accomplished anime writer!

Develop a strong concept

Before you put pen to paper (or fingers to keyboard), it's crucial to have a clear and compelling concept for your anime. Consider the genre, target audience, and overarching themes, as these will help shape the direction of your story. Spend time brainstorming ideas, and don't be afraid to think outside the box to create a unique and engaging premise.

Create memorable characters

Strong, relatable characters are at the heart of any successful anime. As you develop your characters, consider their personalities, motivations, and roles in the story. Create detailed character profiles, outlining their backstories, relationships, and any specific quirks or traits that make them stand out. Remember, your characters are the driving force behind your story, so invest time and effort into creating fully realized, multidimensional characters that your audience will connect with.

Establish a clear structure

A well-structured script is essential for maintaining narrative flow and ensuring that your story unfolds in a logical and engaging manner. Familiarize yourself with the three-act structure, which consists of setup (Act 1), confrontation (Act 2), and resolution (Act 3). Within this framework, you can further break down your story into smaller, more manageable scenes and sequences that propel the narrative forward.

Write compelling dialogue

Dialogue is a critical element of your script, as it brings your characters to life and conveys essential information to your audience. When writing dialogue, focus on creating natural, believable exchanges that reveal your characters' personalities and motivations. Avoid overly expository dialogue and opt for subtlety and nuance, allowing your audience to uncover the story's layers and complexities through character interactions.

Show, don't tell

One of the golden rules of scriptwriting is to show, not tell. In other words, use visual storytelling techniques to convey information and emotions, rather than relying solely on dialogue. Remember, anime is a visual medium, so take advantage of the unique opportunities it offers to create powerful and engaging visual storytelling.

Maintain consistent pacing

Pacing is crucial for maintaining audience engagement and ensuring that your story unfolds at an appropriate tempo. Be mindful of the balance between action, dialogue, and exposition, and avoid lengthy, drawn-out scenes that may cause your audience to lose interest. Keep your script lean and focused, moving the narrative forward with purpose and momentum.

Develop strong themes and motifs

Incorporating themes and motifs into your script can add depth and resonance to your story. As you write, consider the underlying messages and ideas you wish to convey and weave them subtly into your narrative. By incorporating strong themes and motifs, you'll create a more profound and thought-provoking viewing experience for your audience.

Revise and refine

Writing a great script is an iterative process, so be prepared to revise and refine your work multiple times. As you review your script, focus on improving clarity, coherence, and emotional impact. Seek feedback from trusted peers and mentors, and be open to criticism and suggestions. Remember, great scripts are rarely written in a single draft, so embrace the revision process as an opportunity to hone and perfect your storytelling skills.

Format your script professionally

Proper script formatting is essential for ensuring that your work is taken seriously and can be easily understood by collaborators, such as animators, directors, and voice actors.

Familiarize yourself with industry-standard script formatting conventions, including the use of sluglines, action lines, character names, and dialogue. There are numerous screenwriting software options available that can help streamline the formatting process and ensure that your script looks polished and professional.

Collaborate with others

Creating a successful anime is a collaborative process, so be prepared to work closely with others, such as animators, directors, voice actors, and sound designers. Share your vision and goals for the script, and be open to feedback and suggestions from your team. Remember, collaboration often leads to the best results, as it allows for a diversity of ideas and perspectives to shape and enhance your story.

Keep learning and growing

As an aspiring anime writer, it's essential to continually hone your craft and expand your knowledge of the medium. Study the work of successful anime writers and dissect their scripts to gain insights into their techniques and approaches. Attend workshops, join writing groups, and network with fellow writers and industry professionals to learn from their experiences and perspectives. By constantly seeking to improve your skills and understanding of the craft, you'll be well on your way to becoming a successful anime writer.

Develop a thick skin

Writing is a deeply personal and often vulnerable process, and it's essential to develop a thick skin when sharing your work with others. Be prepared for criticism and rejection, and use these experiences as opportunities for growth and improvement. Stay focused on your passion for storytelling and your love of anime, and use this as motivation to keep pushing forward, even in the face of adversity.

In conclusion, crafting the perfect anime script takes time, dedication, and a willingness to learn and grow as a writer. By focusing on developing strong concepts, characters, and dialogue, while mastering the essential aspects of structure, pacing, and visual storytelling, you'll be well on your way to creating captivating and memorable anime stories. So, gather your ideas, grab your favorite writing tools, and let's get started on creating the next anime masterpiece!

Chapter 12: The Business of Anime: Navigating the Industry

Hey there, aspiring anime creators! In this chapter, we'll explore the business side of the anime industry, offering insights and tips to help you navigate this exciting and competitive landscape. From understanding the production process to marketing and distribution, we've got you covered. So, let's dive in and get ready to turn your anime dreams into a reality!

Understand the production process

To effectively navigate the anime industry, it's crucial to have a thorough understanding of the production process. Familiarize yourself with the various stages of anime production, including pre-production (concept development, scriptwriting, character design, etc.), production (animation, voice acting, soundtrack creation, etc.), and post-production (editing, sound mixing, etc.). By understanding the intricacies of the production process, you'll be better equipped to manage your own projects and collaborate with others.

Build a strong portfolio

Whether you're a writer, animator, or voice actor, having a strong portfolio showcasing your work is essential for making a splash in the anime industry. Spend time refining your craft and creating high-quality work that demonstrates your skills and passion. Share your portfolio on your website, social media channels, and industry forums to gain exposure and attract the attention of potential collaborators, clients, or employers.

Network, network, network

Building a strong professional network is critical for success in the anime industry. Attend industry events, conferences, and workshops to meet fellow professionals and learn from their experiences. Join online forums and social media groups to engage with your peers and stay up-to-date with the latest trends and news. Networking not only helps you build valuable connections but can also open doors to new opportunities and collaborations.

Understand the financial aspects

Producing an anime can be a costly endeavor, so it's essential to understand the financial aspects of the industry. Familiarize yourself with the various funding options available, such as grants, sponsorships, crowdfunding, and private investment. Develop a realistic budget for your project, considering costs such as animation production, voice acting, marketing, and distribution. By having a solid grasp of the financial side of the industry, you'll be better prepared to manage your projects and make informed decisions about your career.

Explore collaboration and partnership opportunities

Collaborating with others is a key aspect of the anime industry, and partnerships can offer valuable resources and support. Seek out potential collaborators who share your vision and can contribute their skills and expertise to your project. Partnerships with studios, production companies, or even other independent creators can help you access resources, funding, and distribution channels that might otherwise be out of reach.

Learn about marketing and promotion

Once your anime is complete, it's crucial to effectively market and promote your work to reach your target audience. Develop a marketing plan that includes strategies such as social media promotion, public relations, content marketing, and partnerships with influencers or other creators. By investing time and effort into marketing and promotion, you can increase the visibility of your work and attract a loyal audience.

Understand distribution channels

In today's digital age, there are numerous distribution channels available for sharing your anime with the world. Familiarize yourself with the various platforms, such as streaming services, video-on-demand, and physical media (e.g., Blu-ray and DVD). Research the requirements and submission processes for each platform, and choose the channels that best align with your target audience and goals. By understanding the distribution landscape, you'll be better positioned to get your work in front of viewers and maximize its potential for success.

Protect your intellectual property

As a creator, it's essential to protect your intellectual property (IP) rights to ensure that your work is not used or distributed without your permission.

Consult with legal professionals to understand copyright laws and other intellectual property protections available in your country. Register your work with the appropriate authorities, and be proactive in monitoring the use of your content online. By protecting your IP, you'll be safeguarding your creative work and ensuring that you maintain control over its distribution and use.

Stay informed about the industry

The anime industry is continually evolving, with new trends, technologies, and opportunities emerging all the time. Stay informed about the latest developments by following industry news, attending events, and engaging with your peers. By keeping your finger on the pulse of the industry, you'll be better equipped to adapt to changes and capitalize on new opportunities as they arise.

Develop a long-term career plan

Breaking into the anime industry can be challenging, so it's essential to have a long-term career plan in place. Set clear goals for your career and map out the steps you'll need to take to achieve them. Consider the skills and experience you'll need to develop along the way, and be prepared to invest time and effort into your personal and professional growth. By having a clear vision for your future in the industry, you'll be better prepared to navigate the ups and downs of your career journey.

Be persistent and resilient

Success in the anime industry often requires persistence and resilience, as you may face setbacks, rejection, or even failure along the way. Maintain a positive mindset, and be prepared to learn from your experiences and adapt your approach as needed. Remember that even the most successful creators have faced challenges and obstacles, so don't be discouraged if your journey is not smooth sailing. Stay focused on your passion for anime, and keep pushing forward in pursuit of your dreams.

Seek mentorship and guidance

Finding a mentor or seeking guidance from experienced industry professionals can be invaluable in helping you navigate the anime industry. A mentor can provide insights, advice, and support based on their own experiences, helping you avoid common pitfalls and make informed decisions about your career. Don't be afraid to reach out to potential mentors, either in person or online, and be open to learning from their wisdom and expertise.

In conclusion, navigating the anime industry requires a combination of passion, persistence, and knowledge. By understanding the production process, building a strong portfolio, networking, and staying informed about the latest trends and developments, you'll be well on your way to establishing a successful career in the world of anime. So, go forth and conquer, and let your love for anime fuel your journey through this exciting and dynamic industry!

Chapter 13: Collaborating with Others: Building Your Anime Team

Creating a fantastic anime is often a team effort, with various talented individuals coming together to bring your vision to life. In this chapter, we'll explore how to collaborate effectively with others and build a strong team that can help you achieve your anime dreams. Let's get started!

Define your vision and goals

Before assembling your team, it's essential to have a clear vision and set of goals for your anime project. What kind of story do you want to tell? What is the tone and style of your anime? By having a well-defined vision, you'll be better equipped to communicate your ideas and expectations to your team members and ensure everyone is on the same page.

Identify the roles and skills needed

Next, consider the various roles and skills needed to bring your anime to life. This may include scriptwriters, character designers, animators, background artists, voice actors, composers, and sound engineers, among others. Make a list of the key roles and the skills each team member should possess to ensure your project runs smoothly and efficiently.

Seek out talented individuals

With a clear understanding of the roles and skills needed, you can now begin the process of seeking out talented individuals to join your team. There are various ways to find potential team members, including:

Online forums and communities dedicated to anime, manga, or animation

Social media platforms, such as Twitter, Instagram, or LinkedIn

Networking at industry events, conferences, or workshops

Asking for recommendations or referrals from your existing network

When evaluating potential team members, consider their skills, experience, and passion for the project. It's also essential to assess their ability to work well with others and contribute positively to the team dynamic.

Establish clear communication channels

Effective communication is key to a successful collaboration. Establish clear communication channels for your team, such as email, messaging apps, or project management tools like Trello or Asana. Ensure that all team members have access to the necessary information and resources and encourage open, honest communication throughout the project.

Delegate tasks and responsibilities

As the leader of your anime team, it's crucial to delegate tasks and responsibilities effectively. Assign tasks based on each team member's skills and expertise, and provide clear instructions and deadlines. Be mindful of workload distribution and try to strike a balance to ensure everyone can work efficiently and maintain a healthy work-life balance.

Foster a positive team culture

A positive team culture can make all the difference in the success of your anime project. Encourage a supportive, collaborative environment where everyone feels valued and appreciated. Celebrate successes and milestones, and be understanding and empathetic when challenges or setbacks arise. By fostering a positive team culture, you'll be creating an environment in which everyone can thrive and do their best work.

Provide constructive feedback

Providing constructive feedback is an essential part of the collaborative process. When offering feedback to your team members, be specific, clear, and objective. Focus on the work and the improvements needed, rather than on the person. Encourage team members to share their thoughts and ideas, and be open to receiving feedback as well. A collaborative, feedback-driven environment can lead to higher quality work and a stronger overall project.

Stay organized and manage deadlines

As the leader of your anime team, it's essential to stay organized and manage deadlines effectively. Use project management tools or create a master schedule to track progress, set deadlines, and ensure that everyone is on track. Regularly check in with your team members to address any issues or roadblocks and make adjustments as needed to keep the project moving forward.

Be flexible and adaptable

In any creative project, challenges and obstacles are bound to arise. Be prepared to be flexible and adaptable in the face of unexpected changes or setbacks. Encourage your team members to think creatively and find solutions to problems that may arise. Remember that collaboration often involves compromise and finding the best path forward for the project as a whole.

Encourage collaboration and brainstorming

Fostering a collaborative environment where team members feel comfortable sharing their ideas and brainstorming together can lead to more innovative and engaging anime projects. Schedule regular team meetings or brainstorming sessions to discuss ideas, address challenges, and keep everyone aligned with the project's goals and vision. By encouraging collaboration, you'll be tapping into the collective creativity and talent of your team to create a truly unique and memorable anime.

Acknowledge and celebrate accomplishments

Throughout the project, take the time to acknowledge and celebrate the accomplishments of your team members. Recognize their hard work, dedication, and contributions to the project. Celebrating successes, both big and small, can boost morale and motivation, helping to create a positive and enthusiastic team dynamic.

Learn from your experiences

Every collaboration is an opportunity to learn and grow, both as an individual and as a team. After completing your anime project, take the time to reflect on your experiences and identify areas for improvement or growth. Discuss your team's strengths and weaknesses, and consider how you can work even more effectively together in the future. By learning from your experiences, you'll be better prepared for future collaborations and continue to grow as a creator and leader.

In conclusion, building a strong anime team involves identifying the right talent, fostering a positive and collaborative team culture, and effectively managing the project from start to finish. By following the tips and strategies outlined in this chapter, you'll be well on your way to assembling a powerhouse team capable of bringing your anime vision to life. Remember that collaboration is the key to success, so embrace the power of teamwork and enjoy the creative journey!

Chapter 14: Marketing and Promoting Your Anime

You've poured your heart and soul into creating an amazing anime, and now it's time to share it with the world! In this chapter, we'll explore effective marketing and promotion strategies to help you get your anime noticed and build a dedicated fanbase. Let's dive in!

Identify your target audience

Before you start promoting your anime, it's essential to have a clear understanding of your target audience. Who is your anime aimed at? What age range, interests, and preferences do they have? By identifying your target audience, you can tailor your marketing and promotion efforts to reach the right people and generate interest in your anime.

Create a compelling online presence

In today's digital world, having a strong online presence is crucial for promoting your anime. Start by creating a website or blog dedicated to your anime, showcasing your artwork, character bios, and other relevant information. Make sure your site is visually appealing, easy to navigate, and optimized for search engines.

Social media platforms such as Twitter, Instagram, and Facebook are also excellent tools for promoting your anime. Create engaging content, such as behind-the-scenes looks, sneak peeks, and artwork, to share with your followers. Engage with your audience by responding to comments and messages, and encourage them to share your content with their friends.

Develop a marketing plan

A well-thought-out marketing plan can help you stay organized and focused on your promotional efforts. Outline your marketing goals, target audience, promotional strategies, and timeline in your plan. Be sure to include a mix of online and offline marketing tactics to maximize your reach and visibility.

Network within the industry

Building relationships within the anime industry can be incredibly beneficial when it comes to promoting your work. Attend conventions, workshops, and other industry events to network with fellow creators, producers, and fans. Establishing connections within the industry can open doors to collaborations, sponsorships, and other promotional opportunities.

Collaborate with influencers and content creators

Partnering with influencers and content creators who share a similar target audience can help you reach new fans and generate buzz around your anime. Reach out to bloggers, YouTubers, and social media influencers who cover anime, and propose a collaboration or partnership. This could involve creating content together, hosting giveaways, or featuring your anime on their platform.

Leverage public relations

Getting your anime featured in the media can significantly boost your visibility and credibility. Create a press kit that includes a press release, high-resolution images, and other essential information about your anime. Reach out to relevant media outlets, such as websites, magazines, podcasts, and newspapers, and pitch your story.

Submit your anime to festivals and competitions

Participating in anime festivals and competitions is an excellent way to gain exposure, showcase your work to industry professionals, and potentially win awards or recognition. Research and submit your anime to relevant festivals and competitions, and be prepared to attend and network at these events if your work is selected.

Utilize email marketing

Building an email list of fans and supporters is a powerful way to stay connected and share updates about your anime. Encourage people to sign up for your newsletter through your website, social media, and other marketing channels. Send out regular emails with engaging content, such as behind-the-scenes updates, special offers, and announcements, to keep your subscribers engaged and excited about your anime.

Offer exclusive content and merchandise

Creating exclusive content and merchandise can help you generate additional income while promoting your anime. Design and sell items such as posters, T-shirts, keychains, and other collectibles featuring your characters and artwork. Offer exclusive content, such as bonus episodes, behind-the-scenes footage, or digital artbooks, as incentives for fans to support your project or purchase merchandise.

Engage with your fans

Building a dedicated and passionate fanbase is essential for the long-term success of your anime. Engage with your fans by responding to their comments and messages on social media, hosting live streams or Q&A sessions, and creating content that invites their input and opinions. By fostering a sense of community and connection, you'll be encouraging fans to become advocates for your anime, sharing it with their friends and helping it grow in popularity.

Attend and host events

Attending and hosting events can be a fantastic way to promote your anime and connect with fans in person. Look for local conventions, screenings, or meetups where you can showcase your work, participate in panels or discussions, and network with other creators and fans. Consider hosting your own launch event, workshop, or screening to generate excitement and interest around your anime.

Utilize paid advertising

While many promotional strategies can be executed for little or no cost, investing in paid advertising can help you reach a larger audience more quickly. Consider running targeted ads on social media platforms, search engines, or relevant websites to increase your visibility and attract new fans. Be sure to track the performance of your ads and adjust your strategy as needed to maximize your return on investment.

Monitor your progress and adjust your strategy

Promoting your anime is an ongoing process, and it's essential to monitor your progress and adjust your strategy as needed. Keep an eye on your website traffic, social media engagement, and other key performance indicators to gauge the effectiveness of your promotional efforts. Use this data to make informed decisions about your marketing strategy and focus your efforts on the tactics that are generating the best results.

Learn from others

There's always more to learn when it comes to marketing and promotion, so be open to learning from others in the industry. Follow successful creators and observe their promotional strategies, attend workshops or webinars, and stay up-to-date on industry trends and best practices. By continually learning and adapting your approach, you'll be better equipped to promote your anime and achieve long-term success.

In conclusion, promoting your anime requires a mix of creativity, persistence, and strategic planning. By leveraging a variety of promotional tactics and engaging with your fans, you can generate buzz and excitement around your work and grow your fanbase. Remember that success often takes time, so stay patient and committed to your promotional efforts, and you'll be well on your way to making your anime a hit. Good luck!

Chapter 15: The Future of Anime: Exploring New Horizons

Anime has come a long way since its early beginnings, evolving into a global phenomenon that captivates millions of fans worldwide. As the industry continues to grow and change, new technologies, platforms, and creative approaches are shaping the future of anime. In this chapter, we'll explore the exciting developments and trends that are pushing the boundaries of anime and opening up new horizons for creators and fans alike.

Virtual reality and immersive experiences

Virtual reality (VR) has the potential to revolutionize the way we consume and experience anime. By immersing viewers in fully realized 3D environments, VR can offer a level of interactivity and immersion that traditional anime simply can't match. As VR technology becomes more accessible and affordable, we can expect to see more anime creators experimenting with this exciting medium, crafting immersive stories and experiences that transport viewers to fantastical worlds.

Artificial intelligence and automation

Artificial intelligence (AI) and machine learning are playing an increasingly significant role in the world of animation. AI-powered tools can assist with tasks like in-betweening, color grading, and background generation, speeding up the production process and allowing creators to focus on more creative aspects of their work. As AI technology continues to advance, we can expect to see it play a more significant role in the production of anime, potentially even generating fully automated content in the future.

Streaming platforms and global accessibility

The rise of streaming platforms has had a profound impact on the way people consume anime, making it more accessible than ever before. Services like Crunchyroll, Netflix, and Amazon Prime Video have allowed fans to access a vast library of anime content from around the world, often with subtitles or dubbing in multiple languages. This increased accessibility has not only expanded the global audience for anime but also opened up new markets and opportunities for creators.

Diverse representation and inclusive storytelling

As anime continues to grow in popularity and reach a broader audience, the demand for more diverse representation and inclusive storytelling is also on the rise. Creators are increasingly exploring stories and characters that represent a wide range of cultural backgrounds, gender identities, and experiences, offering fresh perspectives and challenging traditional anime tropes. This trend towards inclusivity and diversity is likely to continue, enriching the anime landscape and making it more appealing to a broader range of viewers.

Cross-media collaborations

Anime has always had a close relationship with other forms of media, such as manga, light novels, and video games. In recent years, however, we've seen an increase in cross-media collaborations that push the boundaries of traditional anime storytelling. Examples include interactive visual novels that blend anime and gaming elements, live-action adaptations that bring anime characters to life, and mixed-media projects that combine animation with live performances. These innovative approaches offer exciting new possibilities for creators and fans alike.

The rise of independent creators and platforms

While major studios have traditionally dominated the anime industry, the rise of digital platforms and tools has made it easier than ever for independent creators to produce and distribute their own anime. Platforms like YouTube, Vimeo, and Newgrounds provide an outlet for indie animators to share their work with a global audience, while crowdfunding platforms like

Kickstarter and Patreon offer a means of securing funding and building a supportive community of fans. As these platforms continue to grow, we can expect to see even more unique and diverse voices emerging in the world of anime.

4K and beyond: The future of animation quality

The ongoing development of display technology, such as 4K resolution and HDR, is pushing the boundaries of animation quality and providing new opportunities for creators to showcase their work in stunning detail. As display technology continues to evolve, we can expect to see anime creators experimenting with new techniques and styles Fan creations and online communities have played a significant role in shaping the future of anime. From fan art and fanfiction to fan-subbing and fan-dubbing, these dedicated communities help to spread awareness of anime and generate new content inspired by their favorite shows and characters. In addition, the increasing popularity of platforms like TikTok and YouTube has allowed fans to create and share their own anime-inspired content, further expanding the reach and impact of the medium. As the line between fan creations and official content continues to blur, we can expect to see even more collaboration and cross-pollination between creators and their fans.

The growing influence of Western animation

While anime has traditionally been associated with Japanese animation, the influence of Western animation has become increasingly prominent in recent years. Shows like Avatar: The Last Airbender, The Dragon Prince, and Castlevania have embraced anime-inspired art styles and storytelling techniques, appealing to fans of both Eastern and Western animation. This blending of styles and cultural influences is opening up new possibilities for creators around the world, enriching the anime landscape and offering fresh perspectives on traditional themes and tropes.

The continued importance of traditional animation techniques

Despite the rise of digital animation tools and technologies, traditional animation techniques, such as hand-drawn cel animation and stop-motion, continue to play a vital role in the future of anime. Many creators and fans appreciate the unique aesthetic and tactile quality that traditional techniques bring to the medium, and some studios, like Studio Ghibli, have even chosen to return to hand-drawn animation in recent projects. As the industry evolves and new technologies emerge, the continued importance of traditional animation techniques is a testament to the enduring appeal and timeless charm of the art form.

Environmental and social awareness in storytelling

As global concerns about the environment and social issues continue to grow, we can expect to see more anime creators tackling these topics in their storytelling. From exploring the impact of climate change and pollution to addressing issues of inequality and discrimination, anime has the power to raise awareness and inspire positive change through compelling narratives and engaging visuals. By tackling these important themes, creators can help to foster a deeper understanding and empathy for the world around us, while also offering viewers a thought-provoking and entertaining experience.

In conclusion, the future of anime is filled with exciting possibilities and new horizons. From the embrace of cutting-edge technologies and platforms to the exploration of diverse themes and storytelling approaches, the medium is continually evolving and pushing the boundaries of what is possible. As creators and fans alike continue to innovate and experiment, the world of anime will no doubt continue to captivate and inspire us for many years to come.

As we wrap up our journey through "Do It Yourself Anime," we hope that this comprehensive guide has inspired, informed, and empowered you to embark on your own creative adventure in the world of anime. From the fundamentals of storytelling and character design to the intricacies of production and marketing, this book has aimed to provide you with the tools and knowledge you need to bring your anime vision to life.

Throughout this guide, we've highlighted the importance of passion, dedication, and perseverance in the pursuit of your creative dreams. Whether you're a seasoned artist or a complete beginner, the world of anime offers endless opportunities for growth, learning, and self-expression. Remember that every great anime started as an idea, and by nurturing and developing your own unique ideas, you too can make a lasting impact in this dynamic and diverse medium.

As you continue your journey, never underestimate the power of community and collaboration. By connecting with fellow creators, sharing your work, and supporting others in their creative endeavors, you'll become part of a thriving and supportive network that can help you reach new heights of success and fulfillment.

Finally, always keep an eye on the ever-changing landscape of anime and stay curious about new trends, technologies, and opportunities. The future of anime is bright, and by remaining adaptable and open-minded, you'll be well-equipped to navigate its exciting twists and turns.

Thank you for joining us on this journey, and we wish you the very best of luck as you embark on your own anime adventure. Be bold, be creative, and most importantly, have fun!

THE END